# PEQUEÑOS DEPORTISTAS

## SPORTS FOR SPROUTS

# Danza
## Dance

### Holly Karapetkova

ROURKE PUBLISHING

Vero Beach, Florida 32964

www.rourkepublishing.com

Photo credits: All photos © Blue Door Publishing except Cover © Leah-Anne Thompson; Title Page © Wendy Nero, Crystal Kirk, Leah-Anne Thompson, vnosokin, Gerville Hall, Rob Marmion; Page 3 © Studio 1One; Page 23 © Blue Door Publishing, MalibuBooks; Sidebar Silhouettes © Sarah Nicholl

Editor: Meg Greve

Cover and page design by Nicola Stratford, Blue Door Publishing
Bilingual editorial services by Cambridge BrickHouse, Inc.      www.cambridgebh.com

Acknowledgements: Thank you to *Heather's Dance Studio* (www.heathersdancestudio.com), Indialantic and Palm Bay, Florida for their assistance on this project

Library of Congress Cataloging-in-Publication Data

Karapetkova, Holly.
  Dance / Holly Karapetkova.
     p. cm. -- (Sports for sprouts)
  ISBN 978-1-60694-323-6 (hard cover)
  ISBN 978-1-60694-823-1 (soft cover)
  ISBN 978-1-60694-564-3 (bilingual)
  1. Dance--Juvenile literature. I. Title.
  GV1596.5.K37 2010
  792.8--dc22

                                              2009002256

Printed in the USA
CG/CG

# ROURKE PUBLISHING

www.rourkepublishing.com - rourke@rourkepublishing.com
Post Office Box 643328 Vero Beach, Florida 32964

**Me gusta bailar.**

I like to dance.

3

4

Yo bailo *ballet*. Llevo una malla, un leotardo y **zapatillas de *ballet***.

I do ballet. I wear a leotard, tights, and ballet shoes.

Me agarro de la **barra**, estiro mis dedos de los pies y me paro derechita.

I hold the **barre**, point my toes, and stand up straight.

Me paro en **primera posición** con mis talones juntitos.

I stand in **first position** with my heels together.

Puedo arrastar los pies, arrastrar y golpearlos a la vez, y dar **brincos**.

I can shuffle, flap, and **hop** step.

13

**Yo bailo *hip-hop*.**
**Llevo mis tenis.**

I do hip-hop. I wear
my sneakers.

Me **congelo**, hago movimientos bruscos y bailo al son de la música.

I **lock**, pop, and move to the music.

**A veces bailo solo. A veces bailo con amigos.**

Sometimes I dance alone. Sometimes I dance with friends.

# ¡Bailar es divertido siempre!

It's always fun to dance!

# Glosario / Glossary

**barra**: La barra es una barra fija en la que las bailarinas se sujetan para mantener su equilibrio. Muchas veces la usan para hacer ejercicios.
**barre** (BAR): The barre is the rail that dancers hold to help them balance. Dancers often use the barre to warm up.

**brincos**: Los bailarines de *tap* dan brincos en diferentes ritmos. Brincan sobre la parte delantera de la planta del pie y luego golpean el piso con el talón para crear dos sonidos con un solo brinco.
**hop step** (HOP STEP): In tap dancing, dancers hop step in different rhythms. Dancers hop on the ball of the foot and then tap down with the heel to make two clapping sounds in one hop.

**congelarse**: Los bailarines de *hip-hop* mantienen diferentes partes de su cuerpo en un solo lugar y luego las sueltan. Por ejemplo, un bailarín puede "congelar" un codo y soltarlo al ritmo de la música.
**lock** (LOK): In hip-hop, dancers hold different body parts in place and then let them go again. For example, a dancer might bend an elbow, hold it in place, and then let it go again in time with the music.

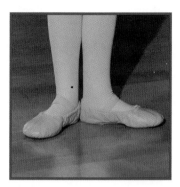

**primera posición**: En la primera posición, una bailarina de *ballet* mantiene juntos sus talones y apunta sus pies hacia fuera.

**first position** (FURST puh-ZISH-uhn): In first position, a ballet dancer presses her heels together and turns out her feet.

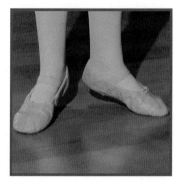

**zapatillas de *ballet***: Son zapatillas especiales que usan las bailarinas de *ballet*. Tienen una suela de piel dura y un tirante sobre la parte superior.

**ballet shoes** (BAL-lay SHOOZ): Ballet shoes are special slippers that ballet dancers wear. They have a stiff, leather bottom and an elastic strap across the top.

**zapatillas de *tap***: Son zapatillas especiales con placas de metal fijadas a la suela. Al bailar suenan como pequeños golpes.

**tap shoes** (TAP SHOOZ): Tap shoes are special shoes with metal plates attached to the bottom. When a tap dancer dances, the shoes make a loud clapping noise.

## Índice / Index

*ballet* / ballet   5

barra / barre   6

brincos / hop step   13

congelarse / lock   16

*hip-hop* / hip-hop   15

malla / leotard   5

*tap* / tap   10

## Visita estas páginas en Internet / Websites to Visit

www.abt.org

www.atdf.org

www.home.howstuffworks.com/dance-activities-for-kids.htm

## Sobre la autora / About the Author

A Holly Karapetkova, Ph.D., le encanta escribir libros y poemas para niños y adultos. Ella da clases en la Universidad de Marymount y vive en la zona de Washington, D.C., con su hijo K.J. y sus dos perros, Muffy y Attila.

Holly Karapetkova, Ph.D., loves writing books and poems for kids and adults. She teaches at Marymount University and lives in the Washington, D.C., area with her husband, her son K.J., and her two dogs, Muffy and Attila.